Dedication

This book is dedicated to everyone who suffers from any form of Mental Health Issue. Well done for getting up every morning and facing the world, even when you do not feel like it. For that, I am proud of you.

I have suffered from Mental Health and Addiction Issues for a very long time and it is important to me that everyone is treated equally and not judged by their Mental Health Diagnosis. There is much more to a person than what they are diagnosed with. I'm hoping this book shows that.

This book has been put together by people suffering from Mental Health Issues and has been done to show the creativity of such people.

I hope you enjoy this collection of creativity.

Jack Griffin

Personal Stories, Poems & Photography

Within this book are sensitive and personal stories told by a few very brave writers about their life experiences and their struggles with Mental Health Issues. These people have been very brave in doing so. Please respect everyone has their own story and these individuals are trying to raise awareness by sharing theirs.

Losing Hope
By Roxy Rafi

Don't lose hope he says,
I look into his eyes and
say I will cope.
He says You need to rest,
I say I'll try my best.
Health is wealth he says,
I say I feel poor in that
aspect.
Don't give into pain he
says, I say don't worry
you don't gain anything
without pain.
He's says you have
something rare, I say
don't you worry I have a
soul that can bare.
I say I will cope as I
leave the room, tears
rolling down my face
just praying not to lose
hope and find a way to
cope by embrace the
things that matter the
most.

I'm Tired
By Jack Griffin

*I'm tired of the lies, I'm tired of the fear. I'm tired of
the truth but it's what I need to hear.*
*I'm tired of the secrets, I'm tired of the drink. I'm
tired of hiding away and hearing what people
think.*
I'm an Alcoholic. What does that really mean?
It means I have an illness, but I wish it was a dream.
I'm tired of falling over, I'm tired of slurring speech,
*I'm tired of missing events and hearing people
preach.*
I'm an alcoholic. What does that make me do?
*It makes me manipulate people. Telling lies to me
and you*
*I'm tired of letting people down and never being
there*
*I'm tired of being so drunk I'm just sat slumped in a
chair.*
I'm an alcoholic that means I drink to live
*I'm tired of the suffering, I've got nothing left to
give.*
Alcohol please let me go and let me live alone
*When I'm craving you, I won't give in I'll be picking
up my phone.*
*Your strength won't win when I share and talk with
others.*
*I'll be sat there sharing in meetings with my sisters
and my brothers.*
*We'll share our experience, strength and hope with
each other*
*We'll share our stories of how tired we are we, so
don't come back, please don't come back, don't you
even bother.*

Feeling Lonely?
By Carol Mogano

If you're feeling lonely,
Here's what you need to do.
Just invite a special friend, to
come and stay with you.

A friend who always love you,
A friend who's always kind.
It's not a living person, its a
friend who's in your mind.

And this friend will forgive
you,
If you ever make mistakes.
Imaginary friends are great,
don't think of them as fakes!

Their love is unconditional,
Just like your mum and dad.
They can tell you everything's
alright, and stop you being
sad.

Mark Phillips Photography

Andy Brown

I was startled awake by an urgent rap on my window. My mind swam reluctantly back to consciousness as I tried to work out why there was an angry-looking man in a high-vis waistcoat knocking on my bedroom window. Moments later, I realised I wasn't in my bedroom: I was in my car. I was cold and I was dreadfully hungover.

'Can you move please?' Said the man outside my window. I mumbled something that may have been 'sorry' and turned my key in the ignition. A policeman might have asked questions about the two empty bottles of merlot in the passenger footwell, or the coil of hosepipe on the back seat. But luckily, the farmer just wanted to know if I could move my car. So, I did, gratefully. And carefully.

This was around six months after my great revelation: the sudden and liberating realisation that I didn't have to be here. Approximately six months before I woke up in my car on a country lane, I made a silent agreement with myself that if things ever got too much, I would take my own life. And approximately 12 hours before I woke up in my car, things finally got too much.

It's difficult to say what triggered the event, but I can say with absolutely certainty that it wouldn't have been anything big; divorce, homelessness, bereavement – these are all things I've coped with reasonably well. More likely, as it so often is, it would have been something small that triggered a train of thought leading rapidly downhill.

Usually, and mercifully, on these occasions, somebody will unwittingly intervene by inadvertently saying the right thing at the right time. But that night, there was no timely intervention: no text from a friend and my girlfriend was fast asleep in her own home. So, my mind was left to spiral unsupervised until I reached the inevitable conclusion: I was a waste of skin and an unfair drain on the resources used to keep me alive. It was time.

Luckily, to make my passing as peaceful as possible, I got good and drunk first. And I woke up some hours later, being shouted at by a farmer and feeling very silly indeed.

That morning, I couldn't countenance the thought of taking my own life; it seemed utterly ridiculous. And yet I knew that the previous night it was the only thing that made sense.

By the time I woke up in my car, I was already receiving counselling, at the suggestion of my girlfriend (now wife – to whom it must be said, I owe a great deal), and it was suggested in a session that I write a letter to my younger self. One of the nuggets of advice I offered my adolescent self was to try harder in school. At 37, it was unlikely I would get the chance to go back to school and try again, but I could go to university, having never been the first time around.

And so, I applied for an undergraduate degree in Creative Writing in Drama, and I haven't looked back since. Having a creative outlet, allied with the enduring support and encouragement of my loving wife has helped me to repaint myself as a valid and valuable member of society with something real to offer myself and the world. I still have the odd 'episode' and I live in constant fear of the grim spectre of that covenant with myself, but the episodes are more infrequent and far less severe, and the world contains more promise now than at any point in my life so far.

Andy Brown

FREEDOM
By Hansa Jethwa

Freedom, oh freedom I yearn thee
What shape and form art thou
My mind boggles
What shape and form art thou.
My mind boggles and questions
Freedom from what?
Freedom to do what?
Freedom from who?
My mind boggles and introspects
Why yearn outside for freedom
When inner mind is shackled
Shackled? Yes shackled
Shackled by fear and thoughts of what others might say
My mind boggles and restricts
Stopping and shackling me from freedom
Freedom, oh freedom I yearn thee
Yes shackled but listening to that yearning within
Yes yearning for that illusive freedom
Yes searching and gathering the speed to attain that freedom
Freedom, oh freedom I come to attain thee.

Mark Phillips Photography

Silence
By Roxy Rafi

Feeling locked in a cage trying to reach for the sky,
Trying to break the Silence that killed my soul slowly every
time, feeling ashamed. And bruised.
How can I tell my story without you being accused!!!!
It wasn't my fault that he thought I could be used as a
victim for him to abuse.
While he felt amused.
Silence burdened my soul heavy, every time scared of being
accused, while my abuse kept him amused.
Finally the silence broke, each bar of the cage came crash
down as the story of my abuse started to unfold.
I'm not the accused, he is, because of my abuse he felt
amused!!!
The bars may build up from time to time,
But at least this bird has tried to fly to reach that blue sky.

Kerry Bestley

What don't kill you makes you stronger.

My name is Kerry, thank you for taking the time to read my story. I would like to tell you about my mental health journey, I was diagnosed with clinical depression, PTSD (post-traumatic stress disorder) and anxiety, when I was 15 years old, this was due to a traumatic childhood which was sexual abuse by my own father, I was placed into care and left there by my birth mother, I was abused physically and emotionally by my foster mother for 10 years where I was also let down by the care system. I was also raped by an ex-boyfriend, which then the trauma left me suicidal, I tried multiple times to commit suicide.

I also suffered domestic abuse from my ex-husband for many years. So, you could say I have had my fair share of trauma in my life. I was left with severe panic attacks in my adulthood. I did try for years to get the right help, but it never happened. I had my son in 2015 but due to postnatal depression I was put on medication. Last year,when out of multiple attempts to ask for help was always told I was too much of a complex case. I finally got the help I needed after searching for so many years. I met my saviour (therapist) and she changed my life I never forget the first time I spoke to her she said to me "I am going to take you by the hand and take you through your journey and I am not going to let go until you want me too" and after 18 months of intense therapy I was able to talk about my story and was able to heal from all the trauma. I never ever gave up trying to search for the right help, even when I felt that I was coming to a dead end.

I am now 41 and I have 2 children and an amazing partner. I am a wellness life coach teaching others how to develop confidence and self-esteem and developing the right mindset to achieve their goals. I also work in education with young people with special needs. I am slowly

14

now coming off my anti-depressants and I have not had a panic attack for a long time. I can now say that I am a survivor of mental health illness. So, the reason I wrote my story is so that if you are struggling with mental health illness don't give up get that help and you never know your saviour like mine will be there waiting for you.

IF I CAN DO IT ANYONE CAN. BECAUSE WHAT DON'T KILL YOU

MAKES YOU STRONGER.

Kerry

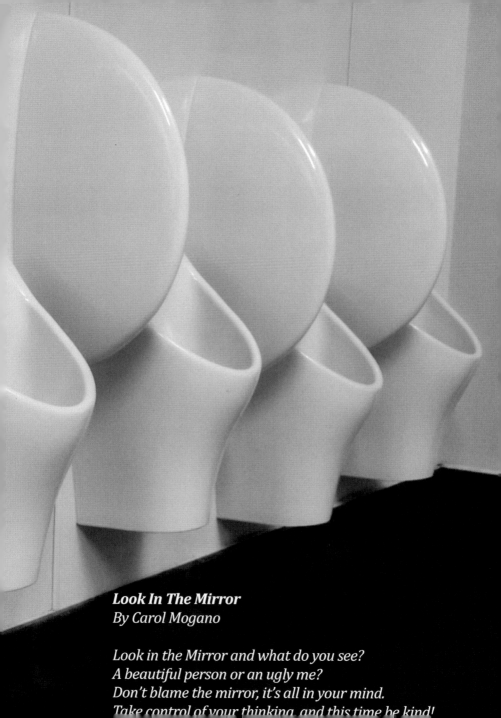

Look In The Mirror
By Carol Mogano

Look in the Mirror and what do you see?
A beautiful person or an ugly me?
Don't blame the mirror, it's all in your mind.
Take control of your thinking, and this time be kind!

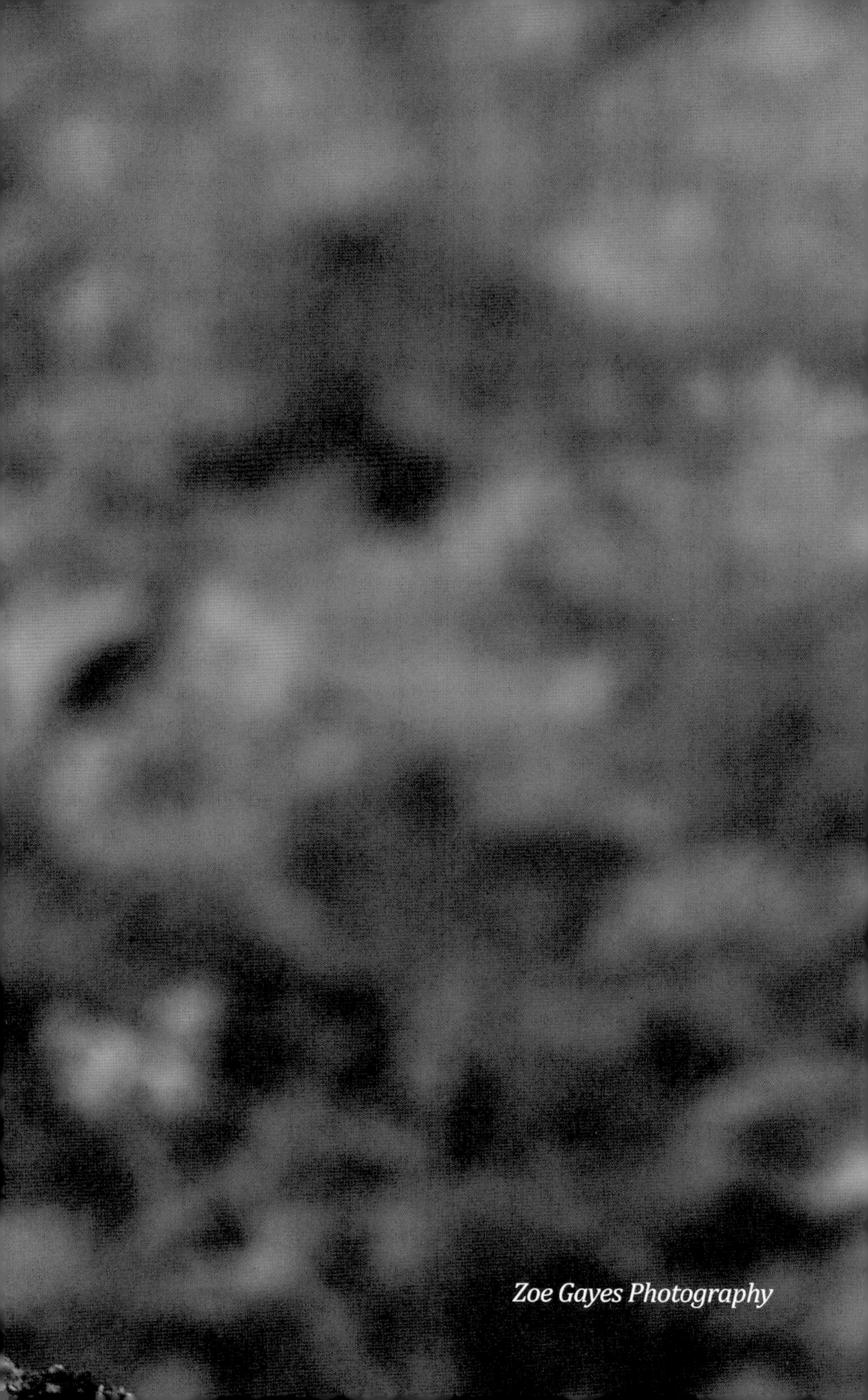
Zoe Gayes Photography

Bill Allsopp Photography

They Come And They Go
By Charlotte Rose Taite

Powerful words
Enough to cut like a knife
Spitting from behind my
teeth
With bite marks and
blood on my tongue
Things I hope not to say,
but do anyway, the shame
If only you knew the battle
in my head to hold in the
thoughts
A tidal wave consuming
my whole being and
gargling in my throat
You say you can handle
my burning soul but you
flinch so soon
I fear that I will always
say too much; am too
much
A rabid animal with a
foaming mouth
And so I just watch you
slip
Slip further away
Goodbye

Mark Philips

My name is Mark Phillips and I am an amateur photographer and for me, photography saved my life. I have suffered with anxiety and depression for 20 years now since losing my mum and within a few months of losing her, I got spiked on a night out which triggered it all. I had tried tablets but couldn't get on with them so I tried another form of help in the way of CBT therapy and my first in house bout I wasn't truthful and only told the doctor what they wanted to hear so it didn't end well.

Two years later (2018) I tried again but this time being referred to Glenfield mental health unit and this time I was honest and put the effort in that was asked from me. It helped me so much as I was unable to eat or drink around others due to the fear of being spiked again and couldn't go far from my home due to the fear of panicking.

With the CBT I was able to venture out and even ate in public, so a massive

achievement, but then it was left to me as they can only help to a certain point.....I was the one that had to continue the journey which is when I decided to take up photography to store memories of the kids and achievements I was making.

Upon receiving the new camera (Nikon d3500) I vowed not to use auto mode as I wanted to learn how to use it properly, so I begun to dive into the books and YouTube tutorials. Slowly but surely I started to improve and before I knew it I was being published in the Leicester Mercury and photography magazines.

Now having my mental health background come in handy slightly during this process as with anyone who suffers mentally will know that you are your own worst critic, so I was always ripping into my own work and then figuring out how I could improve it.

In turn it made me progress rapidly and having OCD also meant I poured everything into photography and strive for perfection if that's even possible. I honestly don't know where I would be without my "medicine" which is photography.

My next battle is to push myself into believing I can turn my hobby into a career as soon as I can, confidence is a massive wall I have to break down but I know ultimately it will improve my future a great deal, so photography is my saving grace.

It's my "happy place" I go to when the days get tough. It gets me out in nature, it gets my creative juices flowing and in turn it releases those critical chemicals (endorphins) that is needed to keep yourself moving forward and not only getting through the day but enjoying it also.

Mark Phillips

My Black Dog
By Matt Green

Always there.
Waiting.
Waiting to pounce.
Debilitating.
Sucking the life from within me.
Frustration.
Oh so much frustration.
Anger.
Anger with myself.
Anger with everyone.
It shouldn't be like this.

I've worked so hard.
I don't deserve this.
Why me?
Why not me?
I've let everyone down.
I've failed again.
No energy.
What's the point?
Am I really an alcoholic?
Surely after all this time it will be different?
Hide.
Hiding away from the world.
Go on.

You can do it.
We've been here before.
Many times
Pick yourself up.
Do the next right thing.
Unisolate.
Pick the phone up.
Connect.
Walk out of that front door.
The black mist is lifting.
I feel better.
I haven't failed.
Depression has never led to the
consequences of drinking.

It is just part of who I am.
Acceptance.
That is the key.
Mental health is just part of who
I am.
Part of being an alcoholic in
recovery.
Take the lows with the highs.
Keep going.
You are worth it.
Don't pick up the first drink.
Then anything is possible.

Bill Allsopp Photography

Recovery
By Ebony Lyons

The things I can do are very few,
I've been struggling now for a
year or two,
Not three or four but many
years more,
Always longing for a life I adore.
My medications help me to
befriend,
The push for recovery to help me
on the mend,
They help my brain to treat me
well,
So I am no longer destined for
hell.
Recovery is so important they
say to me,
But I'm not sure how far I agree,
There is something so comfort-
ing about tearing up my skin,
Yet I no longer let my thoughts
win.
Well fight I must do and on I will
go,
But my brain scares me and my
recovery is slow,
I know that no recovery will
ever be linear,
So why is relapse my biggest,
most desired fear?

Jacqueline Evans Photography

Identity Unknown
By Demi Broughton

Who was she?
Coming to the surface,
From buried deep inside her,
As Adam to Eve,
The forbidden fruit,
You warned me of the darkness.
Took yours, to suit.
Who is she?
I long to know her soon.
As the cries grow louder,
A wolf, to the moon.
One day, confused no more,
A blossomed flower:
For now, I'll wait,
God, give me power.

Nichola Cooley

Finally at Peace

My story is a story full of abuse not just from me abusing myself but mainly from the abuse I received from otherwise.

All my issues started from when I was 11. When you try to speak up to those closest to you about how your feeling and what has happened, just to be shut down, threaten or getting bullied for it. No matter how much you try to get things off your chest and explain what is happening in your world to not being listened to or laughed at. It made me start becoming withdrawn, wanting to find happiness, giving as much love and attention you can to otherwise while showing yourself as a strong person, without a care in the world while mentally you are screaming inside for help and don't know how to get it anymore because I was never heard, I was now at the point I couldn't even share my true feelings to anyone.

My escape by 13 was to cut myself, not because I wanted to die but because I wanted my head to shut up, your not love, your not liked, my body is horrible, no body hears you, you need to be strong, your a failure, you need to show your fake smile, come on girl get yourself together. That all went away as soon as the pain come, everything was finally quiet. I was so happy I finally found so piece (in my eyes I can now cope).

But that only lasts so long, the further you go through life, sexual abuse, physical abuse, mental abuse never seeming to get away from it, it's like life has it in for you and the only way out is for you to take yourself away from that situation. Though that didn't work either as apparently there was something out there keeping me here, keeping me moving forward no matter what fight was put in my path.

Mentally I was a mess, screaming for help wherever I could, people don't see me as having depression and anxiety because I'm a well put together person with a good head on my shoulders, looking after my appearance. No one saw the broken me. The real me.

Alcohol then become my new addiction and oh my it made me feel so much better, my body is light, my head is at peace, I'm dancing, singing, I'm free. Yeah right after a good few months, you get hit like a whole mountain has fallen on top of you, my mental state escalated to the fullest, but I couldn't put that bottle down, I became so angry quickly, I was telling everyone that would listen my past, my pain (how everyday all I feel is pain), doctors/hospital/other professionals now don't listen to you as your not abstinent from substance. If you thought before I was screaming for help it was nothing compared to now. But no one would listen, no one was understanding me, it's just the alcohol talking.

Finally I paid to go into rehab and that where my life changed. I was being listened to, I was being heard, I was getting help. Oh my god I felt safe, from myself and the outside world. Though it was hard being away from my family, it was scary when it was time to come home. But you know I've come home, I get help from mental health services now, I'm still being listened to, I'm getting help thrown at me left right and centre. But you know what the biggest part of all this is? My head is at peace, I know how to manage it now properly. If it wasn't for my parents, close friend and rehab, I wouldn't be here today in control of my life the way I always wanted to be.

Nichola Cooley

If Only
By Leanne Griffin

If only life were different I hear you say
Yet life itself doesn't have to be, only you.
I wish that you could see yourself...as other
see you.

A sensitive, pretty, loving person
Who has all the qualities necessary to
Become a very successful and beautiful lady.

Yet sometimes you seem to have a low
opinion of yourself,
You compare yourself unfavourably...to
others.

I wish that you would only judge yourself
According to your own standards and not be
so hard on yourself.

I look forward to the day when you look in
the mirror,
And see the extraordinary person that you
really are,
And you realize how much you are loved
and appreciate.

I love you so much,
My loyal, trustful companion
Forever as your grateful
friend.

Mark Phillips Photography

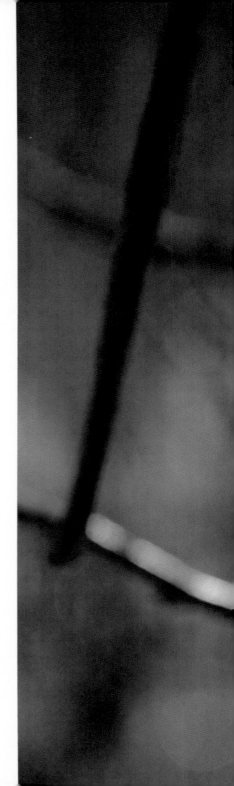

Anxiety
By Kim Dunn

*Dear anxiety cloud, sitting up
there so high
Why don't you let the sun
peep through a bit more
I don't want to feel the cold
sharp rain of self doubt,
Drown in the storm of low
thoughts,
And be blown down by the
suffocating wind
I know there is blue sky, just
let me see it
Bathe in the warmth of the
sun, feel strong & alive.*

34

Blake Davis

Hello everyone,

My name is Blake, I thought I would take the time to write a little bio on myself and who I am.

Starting with the basics, Mental health was and is a huge part of this journey, I grew up in what I thought was a normal family, I lived with both parents who were married, two sisters and a pet dog. We did the "normal" things a family does, it was only when I was spending time with more people like me (performers) that this was not the case, I did not have the support network and safety net from my parents. I grew up with a lack of self-belief, mental strength and self-direction and only ever done things that others wanted and after a while, began to think it was what I wanted. Every day I hated getting out of bed, hated seeing people, making conversation, could not find happiness in anything I did.

Until one day I was saved from all of that, some people may call this lucky, I call it a blessing. A beautiful, strong, caring family took me under their wings saw me and saw that I was more than just another kid, another typical teenager and nurtured me into the man I am today.

Like many others, performing is and always has been a form of escape, another world where I can be and do anything I want and having that has saved me many times.

Performing gives me a sense of freedom and this helped shape me into the man I am today. It helped build confidence, strength and happiness within me, it was after years of graft and failures, took the plunge to go to university and dedicate myself to the one thing that I loved. I then after graduating which I never thought would happen, decided to move away from the "norm" I grew up around and start fresh in another part of the world.

I worked as an entertainer abroad, travelling the world and making the greatest memories, People often saw this as running away.... I saw this as removing myself from an unhealthy and toxic environment and equipping myself with the tools to be able to dilute those things and turn them into a challenge that in time would become so small that it would no longer have a negative influence my life.

With this is mind and learning new ways of approaching situations and developing myself I decided it was time to create a future that I wanted.

Over the past 18 months I have built my own dance school and then worked alongside my partner to create another business that would give other people that feeling of freedom, self-belief and confidence to achieve what they wanted no matter their background, upbringing, sexuality or anything that people struggle with.

Blake Davis

They Call Me Addiction
By Jack Griffin

Hello! It's Me.
They call me 'Addiction'
But I am here to help, I'm here to solve your problems
and numb the pain you felt.
Ill constantly be by your side encouraging you to
drink. Follow what I say, and you will not have to
think.
You won't feel the pain that is deep inside your soul,
I am here to fill the void and that never ending big
black hole.
I promise I'll always be your friend when you are on
your own. I'll take your friends and take your family
and even take your home.
But you'll always have me next to you when you pour
that next large glass. Don't push me away or pity
yourself, all I'll do is laugh.
You need me in your life especially when things are
sad. Don't believe what others say when they tell you
addiction is bad.
All I want in return is for you to dedicate your life to
me. Drink when I tell you, do as I say and I'll make you
happy one day.
Please let me in and destroy your head. Stick with me
and you'll end up DEAD.

Blake Davis Dance

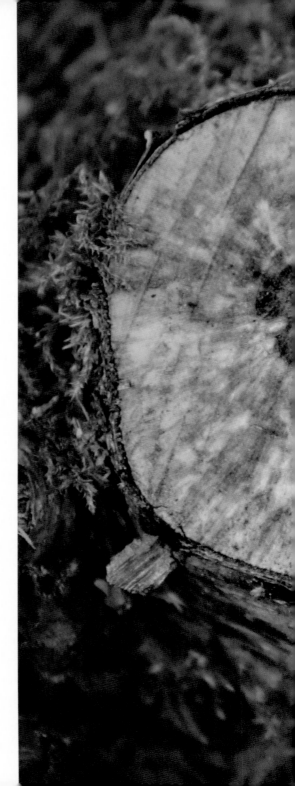

Zoe Gaye

So, my story, like many others who have suffered with their mental health, stemmed from a pretty traumatic childhood. An abusive father, gripped by an addiction to heroin and a mother who was struggling with her own mental health issues, (although I was too young to realise this), culminated in my upbringing being pretty turbulent.

Despite this, my schooling went well and I excelled, until I went to High School. I was really struggling with my mental health – self harming and bulimic. The teachers should have noticed and intervened, yet my form teacher saw how vulnerable I was and abused his position in the worst way possible. My education ended that day. I told no one. My mum wasn't in a position to be able to deal with my trauma and I knew it, so I kept quiet and that's when I turned to drink.

The next few years were filled with recreational drugs, drink and being taken advantage of by predatory men. Then at the age of 19, I met my husband and life started to calm down. He steadied my impulsive side, my recklessness and didn't give in to my constant need for reassurance. We had our first child when I was 21 and I strove to be the very best parent I could possibly be, but in the background the drink still lingered. I had our second child at the age of 24. Two children, a part time job in a school and a bottle of wine to help me relax after work. And then another to help me sleep. Before I knew it, all those years of drinking a staggering amount, finally caught up with me and took a massive hold. 4.30am wake ups, to drink my first bottle of wine so I could function. Tremendous withdrawals if I went without alcohol for merely a couple of hours. My life spiralled out of control and feeling hopeless and lost, I attempted suicide.

After a stint in hospital, I came out and was lucky. I had no amount of help thrown at me, and I took it all. I was fortunate enough to get a place at a detox unit. It was either become totally abstinent or lose everything that meant the most to me.

I came out of detox and filled my days with as much as I could. I bought a cheap camera and decided to document some of the places I had walked and the wonderful wildlife I had seen. Then I yearned to be outside taking more pictures, finding more magical interactions with wild animals. 10 years later and with not a drop of alcohol since, my photography passion shows no signs of easing. My camera has got a lot more expensive but It's my therapy; my go to activity when I'm feeling out of sorts. It takes determination and a certain amount of stubbornness to recover, but by finding a passion, it makes it easier and being outdoors is a huge healer.

Zoe Gaye

Trauma Bond Chronology
By Charlotte Rose Taite

You say hello
I wished you'd run
We push and pull
Toxicity mistaken for fun

You say you care
I don't ask why
Because you think I'm the sun
Piercing through the sky

You say you'll stay
I tell you you won't
Because disease consumes me
Until my very last note

You say goodbye
I knew you would
Because it's harder to learn
Even though you could

You say nothing now
Your life moves on
Because you see
What I've become

You said hello
I begged you to run
Can you see why I'm damaged
Toxic love and painful fun

Autumn Sunflowers
By Andy Brown

The window strikes my head,
and I am awake.
A field of ageing sunflowers
slides past;
Pale yellow, fading brown,
Heads bowed and dying with
the growing autumn chill.
A man staggers drunkenly
down the aisle past the rows
of bobble-heads
Past thirty unseen pairs of
eyes
Thirty lives, thirty smells
Thirty untold stories that
the backs of their heads
cannot reveal.
I close my eyes and think of
the sunflowers
As they must have been in
the summer:
Vibrant and golden,
Sightless faces swaying in
the breeze, like the heads of
passengers on a bus.

45

North York Moor
By Graham Pratt

On the frozen ground hardly a sound
Crop headed fields of wheat bound
Cold grey peat stream slipped away
Small birds swoop up and down at play
Turning minds back to happy times
Little chapel and church bell chimes
Spring then came new lambing game
Two field hands tied the knot next day
Made a home together there to stay
Bridge over marsh rolling valley view
Hot summer gone and autumn flew
Sweet woman with her man ever true
Before winter lush green pastures hew
Now buried beneath thick sleet and hail
Even tough hillside sheep looking pale
Border Collie comes by and pen is full
He shakes off the frost never looks dull
Placed somewhere near drystone walls
Cottage shelters them as heavy snow falls
Working farm an early start when duty calls
On the frozen ground hardly a sound

Demi Broughton

OFF GUARD

Do you know what no one warns you about with mental health? They don't warn you about that feeling of... When people catch you as you fall and how it makes you realise how just not okay you are. The whiplash-like sensation of being caught when you were sure that you were doomed. The guilt is worse, the guilt and then the shame. You didn't believe anyone would be there, you didn't think they'd catch you, you didn't think they'd comprehend just how bad things are, and you are constantly convinced that you've already taken up too much of their time.

The shame, that you found yourself on their radar when you used to be the one that they never had to worry about. The awkward conversations when they call and half-heartedly give you the reason for their call when you know actually they're calling to see if you've decided that you still want to live today. You'll be embarrassed by the amount of times a day that you'll apologise, when there is quite genuinely nothing to apologise for. Though, you won't apologise when you probably should... when the consequences of your bad, impulsive decisions begin to impact the people around you. You'll be too angry, too lost... too desolate to care.

They don't prepare you for the dissociation, the constant need to want to switch your mind off, to simply not exist... just temporarily. Enough time for you to put your mind in a box, and tell it that it can come back out when it learns how to behave and play nice. Each week, you'll promise yourself that this is the week that you don't cry, this is the week that you'll keep making healthy choices. This is the week everything will stop being so confusing, you'll be in your own body for once, rather than watching yourself like a ghost.

Despite the above, one thing that I have discovered to be

true is that these experiences, emotions and thoughts will ultimately force you and shape you to be the most authentic version of you. It will command you to look inside yourself, to make you relentlessly want to be a better version of yourself... because one day you'll snap.

You'll realise that this is enough, you won't accept this struggle for yourself, and you'll start to do whatever you can in order to feel better. It will be messy, it will be hard... but you'll do it. I believe in you.

Demi Broughton

One Drop
By Bill Allsopp

In the water in the fountain
In the deep dark sump
Waiting for the hand of God
The power of the pump

Seven billion drops there are
Just one of which is me
Unnoticed in the scheme of
things
One drop in a swirling sea

One of seven billion drops
Of H2O in strife
How long I linger in the sump
Waiting for a life

In this deep dark place I swirl
Then - so suddenly
A force I feel and off I go
Rocketing and free

Rushing ever upward
Heading heavenly
Then suddenly I see the light
Now I can be me

Sparkling in the heavenly air
Dancing dizzily
And then before I know it
I'm falling helplessly

I tumble down and falling
I drop from layer to layer
Until again I am just one
Lost without a prayer

But on this ride called life
The force again I feel
Through that sump and past
the pump
I will make my life real

And struggling on, swept by
the tide
I fight the sun in vain
Evaporate this water
But I will return as rain

Zoe Gayes Photography

Best Friend - A Poem about Alcohol Addiction
By Jack Griffin

We were best friends from the
moment we met.
We had so much fun,
addiction hadn't started yet.
We went everywhere
together, partying and raves.
It was only then when I
started to crave.
I craved you more each day.
I got down on my knees and
begged you to go away.
But you didn't leave, Best
friends don't.
You started to steal my
dreams and my hopes.
Another drink, another line.
You kept convincing me that I
was doing fine.
When I tried to stop drinking
you would always laugh,
When my back was turned
you always filled up my glass.
Were not best friends! You
don't like me!
Now is the time to leave me
alone and finally let me be.

Dance
By Amy Secker

"Having not grown up in a privileged household, I worked and paid for my own dance training. Dance has always been my escape and following my passion as a full time career has been more fulfilling and reassuring than any other activity or pastime. Dance and performing provides more security than even my personal relationships can. My performance career helps build my own support network which makes me feel stronger in myself!"

Jack Griffin

I have suffered from Mental Health for a very long time. The way I used to deal with my problems was to cover the up with certain behaviours. The main behaviour I used was anger. Whenever I felt unwell I would lash out with anger. I would say things I did not mean and would upset people with this behaviour. Eventually I ended up trying to cover up my Mental Health Issues by drinking Alcohol and using Drugs. I did this for a number of years. At the beginning I could handle how much I drank or used and I found it made me feel better, my Mental Health was controlled finally. I felt normal. But what I did not know is that a terrible downward spiral was beginning.

I began drinking and using an excessive amount. I could not control my drinking or using of drugs. It got to the point where I could not control the quantity of which I used these things. I lost friends, jobs, cars. The list goes on. But still I did not stop what I was doing, it just kept getting worse.

After getting in to numerous amounts of trouble with my employer, friends, family and the law I realised how bad things really were. It was at this time that I checked myself into a Residential Rehab to detox and get treatment for my two addictions. I was there for 5 weeks and I learnt so much about myself and my addiction - more importantly, I learnt how to live clean and sober.

I am not perfect and I have slipped up and made mistakes but what I do now is I try to deal with these things without Alcohol or Drugs. I owe so much to the Rehab and Treatment Centre where I went. I learnt a lot from them and I try to put it in practice every single day.

Jack Griffin

Mindful Exercises

Body Scan Awareness
Daily Gratitude Journal
Self Loving & Kindness Meditation

Being aware of your own emotions, recognising them and practising positive enforcement is important to maintaining a healthy mental space. Here are some mindful exercises you can use to help improve your mind space

Body Scan Awareness

Body awareness scan is when we pay attention to parts of our body in a gradual sequence from feet to top of the head by mentally scanning each area. This practice is done by you by bringing your awareness to parts of the body in sequence.

Body awareness scan helps to relieve stress and strengthens the link between the mind and the body. Practice this laying down on your back, feet slightly apart relaxed and arms by your side palms facing upwards and relax the whole body. I personally prefer to do the body awareness scan just before I fall sleep, this helps my body and mind to be in a complete relaxed state. Start off by softly closing your eyes, slowing the breathing down, letting your abdomen expand and contract with each breath, nice slow deep inhales and exhales for a minute or so.

Start the body awareness scan from the feet, pausing for a few seconds before moving onto the next part. Up to ankles, calves, knees and so on and so forth all the way up to the top of you head. Scan your entire body. Are there any areas that have discomfort, aches, pains or tension? If there are any areas with this continue to breathe into these areas and visualise it leaving your body through your breath into the air. Move on to the next when you feel you are ready.

When you have completed releasing bring your awareness back to your breath, nice slow deep inhales and exhales for a moment or so to end the body awareness scan practice.

By Indy Samra

Daily Gratitude Journalling

I was introduced to gratitude journalling some years back. Practicing gratitude can support in reducing stress and anxiety, increase positivity and improve self- esteem. I thought I would share with you how I practice this. Purchase a new small A5 note book, some felt tips, colouring pencils and a nice new pen to write with. Find a time of day daily where you can take 10 minutes out for yourself. Sit silently with your eyes gently closed.

Take a few deep breaths in and out, focusing on your breath. Placing your hand on your heart and chest area, say silently to yourself 'thank you, thank you, thank you.'

Next open your note book and start with the words 'I am truly grateful for' then finish the sentence. Try to write down at least five things you are grateful for daily.

Some of my examples are 'I am truly grateful for my home it keeps me safe and warm, I am truly grateful for my hands so I am able to type this article, I am truly grateful for the food shopping I did this morning, I am truly grateful for my warm lunch I had, I am truly grateful for the opportunity to be a part of this booklet, I am truly grateful to the stranger who smiled at me today'.

As well as listing the gratitude you can try writing 'I am truly grateful for' in the middle of the page and draw pictures for each gratitude. Be as creative as you like with your gratitude journal. Use felt tips and colouring pencils. You can journal and express your gratitude in whichever way is natural to you. I recommend you try gratitude journalling practice and see the benefits for yourself.

By Indy Samra

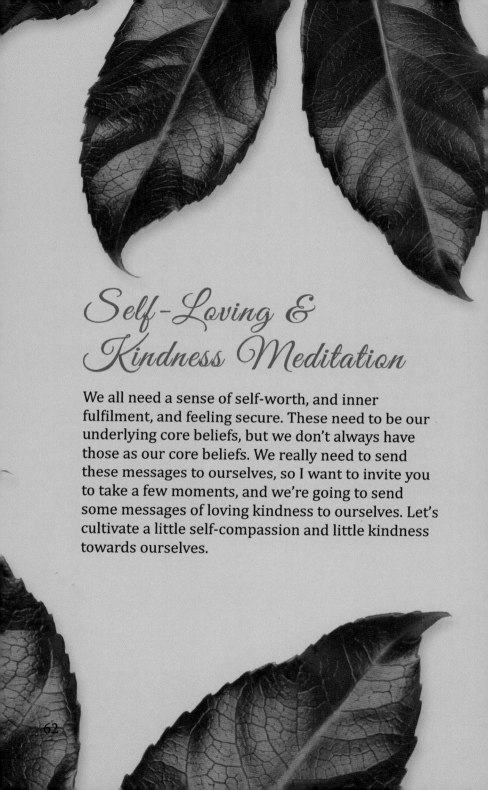

Self-Loving & Kindness Meditation

We all need a sense of self-worth, and inner fulfilment, and feeling secure. These need to be our underlying core beliefs, but we don't always have those as our core beliefs. We really need to send these messages to ourselves, so I want to invite you to take a few moments, and we're going to send some messages of loving kindness to ourselves. Let's cultivate a little self-compassion and little kindness towards ourselves.

Find a nice quiet space where you won't be disturbed for a few minutes.

Take your attention to your breath, no need to change the rhythm of your breath. Become more and more relaxed with each breath. Maintain your breathing at its own natural pace.

Repeat the following phrases silently in your own mind.

May I be safe, and protected........

May I be healthy and strong.........

May I experience love and joy......

May I live my life with ease.....

And may I be at peace......

Take three nice deep breaths in and out then return to your natural normal breathing rhythm. Focus your attention on your heart centre. Our heart is the centre of love, compassion, and joy. Knowing we can always return to that place. Repeat a few times the following silently in your own mind, I am enough and I am loved. Whenever you feel ready, gently open your eyes and bring your awareness back into your room.

I hope you enjoyed this short yet delightful meditation.

By Indy Samra

Borderline Personality Disorder

BPD is a very complex, often misconstrued & highly stigma-
tized mental disorder. People with BPD frequently experience
intense emotional hypersensitivity, and it can be an extremely
slow return to a stable mood again.

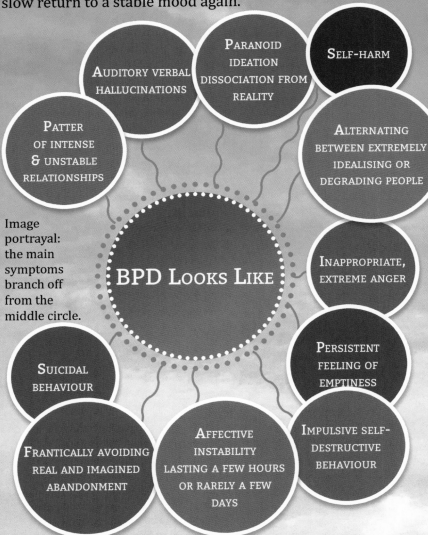

Image
portrayal:
the main
symptoms
branch off
from the
middle circle.

These are the chronic feelings you can experience having BPD. These
are the negative symptoms anybody with BPD has to deal with.

Living with BPD can be like trying to balance and emotional light switch between on and off. It is important to hold into the positive qualities and experiences. In my personal experience this helps keep my feet firmly on the ground, remain balanced, have a fuller picture of life and who I actually am as a person.

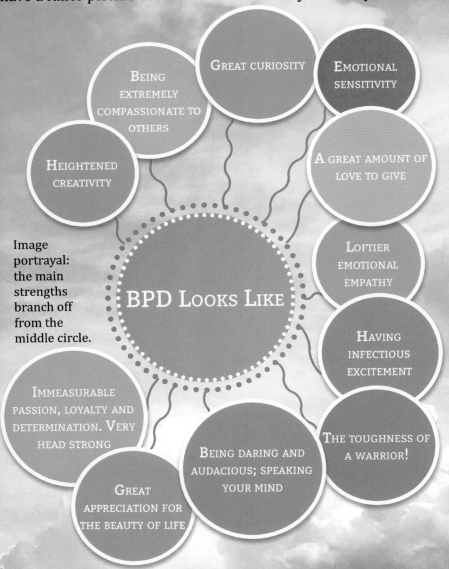

Image portrayal: the main strengths branch off from the middle circle.

These are the more positive attributes of BPD. Showing how much love, compassion, empathy and so much more.

mind

*All money raised from this book will go to MIND
- The Mental Health Charity.*

*Thank you purchasing this book, by doing this
you are helping those who suffer from mental
illness along with the family and friends of them
too.*

I have set up BOOKS 4 THE MIND to help those suffering with Mental Health Issues.

We collect self-help style and positive books and give them to Mental Health Units and Mental Health Services to help those suffering.

To find out more, please visit our Facebook Page: BOOKS 4 THE MIND - Restart Midlands.

Jack Griffin

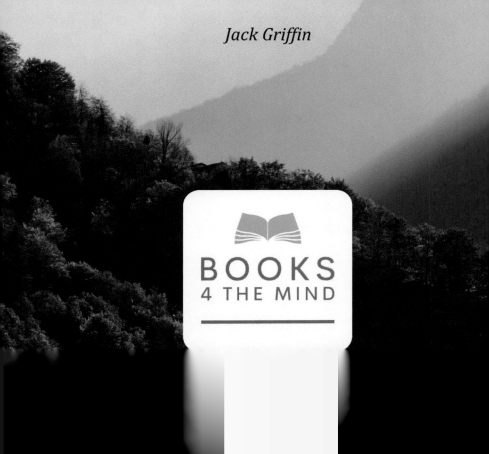

BOOKS

4 THE MIND

Printed in Great Britain
by Amazon